D1435655

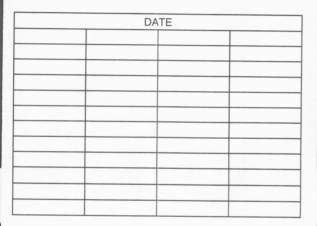

DATE			

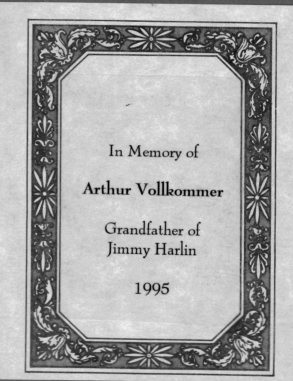

In Memory of

Arthur Vollkommer

Grandfather of
Jimmy Harlin

1995

Parenting Papas

Unusual Animal Fathers

Judy Cutchins
and
Ginny Johnston

Morrow Junior Books   New York

Acknowledgments

We wish to thank the following specialists for their help in the development of *Parenting Papas*: Beth Stevens, Ph.D., and Karen Kearns, Zoo Atlanta, Atlanta, Georgia; Anne Savage, Ph.D., Roger Williams Park Zoo, Providence, Rhode Island; Michael Mahony, Ph.D., University of Newcastle, New South Wales; Dwight Kuhn, Dwight Kuhn Photography, Dexter, Maine; Sally Love, Smithsonian Institution Insect Zoo, Washington, D.C.; Laura Snoeberger, Miami Seaquarium, Miami, Florida; Georgann Schmalz, Robert Connell, Lawrence A. Wilson, Ph.D., and Fred Sherberger, Ph.D., Fernbank Science Center, Atlanta, Georgia.

Photo Credits

Permission for the following photographs is gratefully acknowledged: Animals Animals © 1994 by David Thompson, pp. 12, 14; Animals Animals © 1994 by Harold E. Wilson, p. 38; Chip Clark/courtesy of Smithsonian Institution's Insect Zoo, p. 17; Fernbank Science Center, p. 5; Renée Godard, p. 24; Julie Habel/First Light, p. 33; Thomas Kitchin/First Light, p. 32 (top); Dwight Kuhn, pp. 13, 16, 18; Brian Milne/First Light, pp. 30, 32 (bottom); Leanne Pattinson, pp. 19, 21, 22; Stephen Rasé/Zoo Atlanta, p. 27; Anne Savage, Ph.D., p. 35; Georgann Schmalz, pp. 25, 28; Tom Sullivan/Sullivan Productions, p. 37; Paul A. Zahl/National Geographic Society, pp. 8, 9. The photograph on page 26 is by Judy Cutchins.

The text type is 16-point ITC Berkeley Old Style Book.
Book design by B. Gold/LOGO STUDIOS

Library of Congress Cataloging-in-Publication Data
Cutchins, Judy.
Parenting papas: unusual animal fathers / Judy Cutchins and Ginny Johnston.
p.   cm.
Includes index.
ISBN 0-688-12255-8 (trade)—ISBN 0-688-12256-6 (library)
1. Parental behavior in animals—Juvenile literature.   2. Males—
Juvenile literature.   3. Sexual behavior in animals—Juvenile
literature.   [1. Parental behavior in animals.   2. Animals—Habits
and behavior.   3. Animals—Infancy.]
I. Johnston, Ginny.   II. Title.
QL762.C88   1994   591.56—dc20   93-27014   CIP   AC

Contents

Care of Eggs and Young

A female garden spider, swollen with eggs, hangs in her web. Her eggs were fertilized by a male garden spider that came to the web earlier to mate with her and then left. The female presses her abdomen into the silken sac she has made and deposits a hundred eggs inside. After sealing the sac with more silk, she hides it in a nearby bush, and then she leaves. Neither the mother nor the father spider gives any attention to the eggs or to the young. When the spiderlings hatch, they will be on their own.

The female garden spider wraps her eggs in a tough sac of silk.

In all animal species, it is the female that produces the eggs. But eggs will not develop and hatch unless they are fertilized by sperm from a male of the same species. Producing eggs that will develop into healthy young is the most important job that adult animals have. The young grow up to become adults and parents themselves. As generation follows generation, the species continues.

Most animals in the world are egg layers. Very few of the parents remain with their eggs. Many eggs do not hatch because they are discovered and eaten by predators. Others do not hatch because the weather is too wet or too dry. Fortunately, animals often lay large numbers of eggs. Even if some eggs don't hatch, others do, and the species continues.

For certain kinds of animals, the eggs or young need attention to survive. In these cases, either or both parents have a much greater role in their offspring's lives. Mother mammals, whose young are born alive, remain with their babies to nurse them. Hatchling birds are often brought food by both parents. In other cases, father animals may bring food to mothers that are busy with eggs or young. Some papas remain with their families to train and protect growing offspring.

Certain father animals have more unusual parenting duties. Care-giving males may build nests or incubate eggs without any help from their mates. A few fathers even carry the eggs until they hatch. *Parenting Papas* describes the important roles that seven very different father animals play in the lives of their offspring.

Dwarf Sea Horse

The male dwarf sea horse, no bigger than a paper clip, curls his tail tightly around a stem of sea grass in the warm Florida ocean. His tough, bony skin is exactly the same yellowish green as his grassy home. Amazingly, sea horses can change colors, from yellow to green or even orange, to blend into the coral and grass that grow on the sandy bottom.

Usually the male dwarf sea horse uses this camouflage to hide quietly in his shallow ocean habitat. But on this sunny April day, he is not trying to hide from his enemies. Instead, this unusual fish is showing off to attract a mate. A pocketlike pouch on the front of his body is filled with water and bulges out like a tiny balloon. The father sea horse will brood the eggs of his mate in this pouch until they hatch. He sways with the sea grass and waits for a female to approach.

Nearby, a female dwarf sea horse is feeding hungrily on shrimp larvae. She sucks in a thousand tiny sea creatures like these each day with her tubelike snout. Although her back fin is beating rapidly, she swims forward very slowly. Sea horses are the slowest-swimming fish in the world. At top speed, most move only a foot or less in one minute.

Attracted by the male, the little female uses the fins on each side of her head to turn toward him. Her body is full of eggs, and she is ready to mate. She settles next to the male and twists her tail around a piece of coral. With their bodies touching, the female pushes a special egg-laying tube into the male's pouch. Then she releases three dozen eggs through the tube.

The male fertilizes the eggs as they enter his pouch. When the female

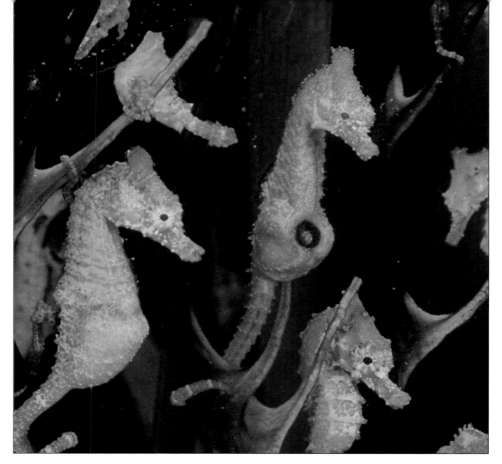

The dark, round opening of the brood pouch widens as the father dwarf sea horse gives birth.

has finished releasing her eggs, she withdraws her tube and slowly swims away. Her job as a parent is complete, but his has just begun.

Soon after the male and female have mated, the father sea horse's pouch closes with the eggs safely inside. For about two weeks, he stays hidden in the sea grass as the eggs in his pouch develop. Blood vessels in the sea horse's body carry oxygen and nutrients to the pouch, where they are absorbed by the eggs. This is necessary for the eggs to develop. As the babies grow, the pouch gets larger.

Finally the father sea horse is ready to deliver his babies. His muscles jerk suddenly, and his whole body strains. The pouch opens and one tiny sea horse pops out, headfirst. It is so small it can barely be seen. For a few seconds, the newborn drifts in the water. Then its little back fin begins to beat, and the youngster swims away.

After a minute's rest, the father's body begins to twitch again. Out comes another hatchling and then another. For nearly three hours, the delivery process continues.

Each youngster swims away and wraps its tail around a piece of seaweed or coral. Before long there are several different colors among the newborns

Popping out headfirst, this tiny baby sea horse will soon swim away on its own.

as their bodies change to match their first hiding places. Each of these dwarf sea horses is on its own. Not one will have any other contact with its parents.

Although the male is exhausted, he will soon recover his strength. By the end of the summer, he may mate and deliver young two more times. The large number of hatchlings is important because most will not survive. Tiny sea horses are eaten by fish, crabs, and eels that hunt in the sea grass. But those that escape their enemies grow quickly. In two or three months they will be fully grown and ready to be parents themselves.

There are about two dozen species of sea horses in the oceans of the world. Most of them are rarely seen because of their quiet life-styles and super camouflage. All sea horses begin life inside the pouch of their father. The dwarf sea horse, with only a one-year life span, is the smallest. This species lives in the Atlantic Ocean off the coast of Florida and in the Gulf of Mexico.

Three-Spined Stickleback

A brilliant afternoon sun beams down on the New Jersey lake. Days are growing longer and warmer as summer approaches. In the lake's deep water, tiny three-spined sticklebacks are camouflaged by their blue and silver colors. Chemicals called hormones in the fish trigger important changes. They cause female sticklebacks to grow plump with eggs. Hormones also cause male sticklebacks to change colors when it is time to attract a mate. Their normally silver-colored underside turns a brilliant orange-red.

Both males and females swim toward the warmer water near the shore of the lake. Each male selects a sandy place in the quiet, shallow water.

While defending his territory, the male stickleback goes to work building his nest. He whisks out a smooth, sandy pit with his pectorals, or bottom fins. Then for three days, the little fish collects bits of algae and shapes them into a nest. After gathering enough algae, the male swims back and forth over the nest, releasing a waterproof glue produced by his kidneys. The glue holds the nest together.

To complete his nest, the male swims straight through the middle. He makes a tunnel that is open at both ends. Just an inch or two long, the nest tunnel is now ready for a female to enter and lay eggs.

When a possible mate approaches, the male stickleback does a zigzag courtship dance. If the female is ready to lay her eggs, she swims inside his nest. After laying three or four whitish eggs, she is nudged out by the male as he swims through the nest and fertilizes the eggs. For a day or two, the male may continue to attract other females to lay eggs in his nest.

The three-inch-long male stickleback carries threads of algae to build his nest.

Mother sticklebacks produce dozens of eggs. Often a female enters more than one nest and leaves a few eggs with different fathers. Each egg has a yolk that will nourish the youngster while it is developing and for a few days after it hatches. Once a mother stickleback's job of egg laying is done, she does not return to any of the nests or see her young.

The father, however, has more work to do. Besides nest building, his job is to watch over the eggs. For two weeks, the male guards his nest fiercely. He fans oxygen-filled water through the tunnel with his fins. He repairs any damage to the nest. Nest guarding is a full-time job, and the father does not leave, even to eat. No animal is allowed to come near the nest. If a hungry fish approaches, the father stickleback swings the spines on his back like a sword and bites the intruder to chase it away. Even females are chased away by the male now that he is guarding his nest.

At last, hatching day arrives. The first of the fry, or hatchlings, breaks out of its egg. As the babies begin to hatch, the father tears away the threads of algae that cover the nursery.

The tiny hatchlings stay together in the nest for a few days. Because the yolk attached to each baby's body is still providing food, the young fish do not need to eat. If one of the fry straggles away, the ever-watchful father grabs it with his mouth and spits it back into the nursery.

After a few days, the male stickleback no longer has the energy to guard so carefully. However, by now the hatchlings are ready to be on their own. One by one, they leave their sandy nursery.

The male stays close by while the female deposits her eggs in the algae nest.

Ever watchful, the father stickleback attacks an algae-eating snail that comes too close to his nest.

Sticklebacks are found throughout the Northern Hemisphere. The various species are identified by the number of spines they have on their backs. For many fish that nest close to shore, it is the male that builds and guards the nest.

Giant Water Bug

A male giant water bug flies down to a pond in the Illinois woods. He folds his wings across his back as he lands on a clump of floating water plants. Then he dives toward the muddy bottom, paddling smoothly with his strong flattened back legs. A thin film of air trapped by microscopic hairs on his body allows him to breathe underwater. Even though he can stay under a long time, the water bug must surface occasionally for more air. Many underwater insects breathe in this interesting way.

Spring is egg-laying time for many of the animals in the pond. And the giant water bug is no exception. When a female swims nearby, the male puts on a courtship display. It looks as if he is doing push-ups underwater!

If the female approaches, the male grasps her with his front legs and fertilizes her eggs. The female then climbs onto the back of her mate and lays almost a hundred eggs. It may take her several hours to finish laying them all. As she releases her eggs, she also releases a very sticky glue. Each egg, smaller than a grain of rice, is stuck firmly to the top of the male's folded wings.

Insects usually give no attention to either their eggs or their young. Many produce dozens of eggs at one time and abandon them. Very few eggs hatch into youngsters that survive to become adults. Predators and other natural hazards destroy eggs and tiny young. This species of giant water bug, however, has adapted a special way of placing its eggs in a very safe place. Instead of leaving the eggs unattended, the father carries them wherever he goes. This may increase the chances of the eggs hatching.

Covered with eggs, the father water bug clings to the leaves of a water plant.

When the father giant water bug is carrying eggs, he spends much of his time at the pond's surface, clinging to plants. Even though giant water bugs usually stay in the deeper parts of the pond, the father holds the eggs near the surface, where they get more oxygen.

After twelve days, the first nymph hatches. It looks exactly like a tiny copy of its parents, but it has no wings. The nymph clings to its father's back for a short time before swimming away on its own. In just a few hours' time, all the young hatch and head for hiding places among the water plants. Soon the empty egg mass falls off the father's back. He may mate again and carry another female's eggs.

By the end of summer, many water bug nymphs have hatched in the pond and gone off on their own. A large number of them are eaten by young salamanders or fish. The youngsters that escape and find enough food for themselves grow quickly.

Each time a nymph molts, or sheds its tough outside skeleton, its body and wings get larger. A water bug nymph molts five or six times before it is fully grown. When it molts for the last time, its wings are fully developed. Then the giant water bug can fly to another pond, where it will search for food or seek a mate, just as its parents did.

There are twenty kinds of giant water bugs living in ponds across North America. A few species lay eggs on plant stems just above the water. Most kinds lay eggs on the back of the father. Giant water bugs are over an inch

After two weeks on the father's back, water bug eggs begin to hatch.

long. They are fierce predators with sharp beaks. These pond hunters eat only live prey: tadpoles, fish, and other insects. They even kill frogs and salamanders that are larger than they are. Although adults can fly, most water bugs stay in the pond where they hatched unless they cannot find enough food.

The dark eyes of a hatching water bug see the world for the first time.

Hip-Pocket Frog

From under the damp fallen leaves on the floor of the Australian rain forest, a male hip-pocket frog calls. It is springtime, and he is seeking a mate. A female leaves her hiding place beneath a nearby log and hops toward the calling male. His calls attract her and also tell his neighbors that this part of the forest is his territory. These tiny frogs are only as big as a man's thumbnail. Their size and grayish brown color camouflage them in the leaf litter.

As the male hip-pocket frog calls for a mate, his vocal sac extends like a yellow balloon.

When the female selects the male as her mate, he grasps her tightly and holds on until she lays a mass of eggs. It may take her as long as nine hours. As she releases the eggs, she also releases a liquid that dries to form a protective cover for the egg mass. As the female deposits the clutch, the male releases sperm over the eggs. About eighteen round white eggs are clumped together in the egg mass.

Both the mother and father frog stay close by to keep a watchful eye on the developing eggs. But even so, a hungry beetle attacks the egg mass. In a few minutes, it bites through the tough protective covering and eats two of the eggs. When the male frog hops toward it, the beetle crawls away. The rest of the eggs are safe.

After eleven days, the eggs begin to hatch, and the tadpoles, or larvae, wiggle inside the egg mass. With her guarding duties over, the mother has finished her job. But now the father hip-pocket frog has very important work to do. He climbs up on the clutch of eggs and, scientists believe, secretes a mucus that softens the tough covering of the egg mass. Where his body touches the covering, it turns to a jellylike liquid.

The tadpoles inside have not yet developed eyes, but they have well-developed tails. A tadpole twitches its tail and wriggles through the jelly mass toward its father's body. It slides into one of the brood pouches located near its father's back legs. These pouches, one on each leg, have tiny slits for openings. Since the pouches open near the hip joint, the frog is called the hip-pocket frog.

After almost twelve hours, most of the tadpoles have squirmed their way into their dad's brood pouches. He then hops slowly away from the egg mass.

The father hip-pocket frog climbs onto the egg mass as the tadpoles begin to hatch (above).
Though blind, the white tadpoles use their strong tails to squirm toward their papa's brood pouches,
or hip pockets (below).

Now the father frog stays hidden on the rain forest floor. He feeds on insects and worms under the fallen leaves. Over the next several weeks, the tadpoles will develop into froglets. Their nourishment comes from the egg yolks that are still attached to their bodies. Each tadpole develops eyes and legs, and its white skin changes to a splotchy brown.

A froglet just out of the pouch rests on its father's back. In a few seconds, the baby will hop away.

After seven weeks, the father frog's pouches are bulging with squirming froglets. It is not long before the first froglet squeezes out of a hip pocket and hops away on its own. Other tiny froglets leave, one at a time, during the next several days, until the last one is gone. The father frog has finished his parenting duties! The new frogs must find their own food and hide from predators if they are to survive in the rain forest.

The hip-pocket frog is the only frog species in which the male has developed pouches that are used only for brooding young. This unusual behavior is a wonderful adaptation for this rain forest frog. If the egg mass were left on the ground while the froglets developed, few, if any, would emerge. The egg mass would dry out if there was not enough rain or wash away if it rained too hard. Hungry predators might eat all the eggs. Bush turkeys or bandicoots might destroy the clutch as they scratched the ground in search of food. But these hazards are overcome by the hip-pocket frog father's special care.

Chilean Flamingo

The female flamingo has been on the nest all night, incubating her single egg. From time to time, she rolls the egg over to warm it evenly. At dawn, the male flamingo approaches, squawking softly. It is his turn to be the nest-sitter. Like many bird species, flamingos choose lifetime mates that share the important nesting jobs.

The mother bird stands, stretches, and steps off the nest. Now she will fly to the shallow lake nearby to search for food. More than ten thousand Chilean flamingos are in this colony on the banks of a South American lake. Each spring they return here to nest.

Not far from their nests on the bank, Chilean flamingos feed in the shallow water of this South American lake.

Cone-shaped nest mounds of thousands of flamingos crowd the muddy bank.

The papa folds his long legs under him and wriggles his body until the egg is nestled close. He reaches his long snakelike neck over and touches bills with a nesting neighbor before tucking his head under his wing to sleep.

Together, the mother and father flamingos built the nest by scooping beakfuls of mud and plastering it down with their beaks and webbed feet. When the nest was finished, the female laid an egg in a shallow depression on top. For thirty days, the parents have taken turns incubating the egg.

The father flamingo turns the egg so that it is warmed evenly while he incubates it.

On a sunny summer morning while the father is nest sitting, he feels the egg move a little beneath him. Tiny peeps can be heard from inside the egg as the flamingo chick begins to hatch. The father talks to his baby by honking. The youngster pecks at the shell and makes a tiny crack. The father rolls the egg so the crack faces upward. This will make it easier for the baby flamingo to break out. For the rest of the day, the crack grows larger. The honking and peeping conversation continues until the baby at last pecks its way free.

Weak and limp, the hatchling lies still in the nest. The young flamingo does not look very much like its parents. Its feathers are soft, and they are not yet pink.

At the end of the day, the mother returns to the nest. Then the hungry father bird leaves to feed. He wades in the shallow water of the nearby lake and pulls his oddly bent beak along the muddy bottom. Its strainerlike edges trap tiny plants and shellfish.

This two-day-old chick is being fed a fat-rich liquid of partially digested food. Both parents feed the baby in this way.

This ten-day-old chick will soon join many others in a nursery group.

The parents continue to take turns nest sitting and hunting for food. Now, instead of an egg to incubate, they have a tiny chick to feed and keep warm and safe from predators. Every few hours, whichever flamingo is feeding returns to the nest to feed the chick. The parent dribbles a fat-rich red liquid made of partially digested food from its mouth into the beak of the hungry youngster.

Just five days after hatching, the young flamingo can run and swim. After two weeks, the new chicks in the colony form a large group. A few adult flamingo "aunties" that do not have chicks of their own baby-sit the youngsters. This allows both the mother and father birds to leave in search of food at the same time.

The nursery group may have a thousand or more chicks. But finding its own young is no problem for a parent flamingo at feeding time. The adult bird, honking loudly, approaches the group. The baby immediately begins calling and runs hungrily toward its parent. Amazingly, each little bird can identify the call of its own parents.

For a few weeks, the chick's beak is straight, not bent like those of the adults. Until the beak changes, the youngster continues to be fed by the parents.

Before winter, the young flamingo's wings will grow stronger, and flight feathers will grow into place. A pinkish pigment in the tiny water creatures eaten by flamingos is absorbed by their bodies and gradually colors their feathers pink. In time, the youngster's feathers will turn the beautiful color of its parents' as it eats more and more of the same type of water creatures.

The adults migrate to warmer shores late in fall, leaving the young flamingos on their own. Days later, the chicks migrate, too. By age four, the chicks will be adults, old enough to choose mates and build their first nests.

There are six species of these brightly colored birds in the world. Most live near warm, shallow waters of tropical countries. The Chilean flamingo is seen in the highlands of Chile, Peru, and Argentina. Colonies may be enormous, sometimes having a million birds.

Red Fox

The March sky is deep purple as the sun sets on the Alabama farmland. In the wintry forest on the far side of a pasture, the night is still and quiet. Beneath a thicket of blackberry brambles at the edge of the forest, all is not so still. In a den dug beneath a rotting tree stump, a female red fox moves restlessly. In just a few hours she will give birth. Outside the den, her mate sniffs the air. For the past few weeks, much of his attention has been devoted to the care of the mother-to-be. As her body grew heavy with pups, she

The male red fox guards and brings food to his mate when she is about to give birth.

hunted less. At night the male caught mice, rabbits, and other small prey for both of them.

Throughout the night, the female turns uncomfortably inside the den. By dawn, five helpless pups with eyes tightly closed are born. The mother remains inside the den, nursing the newborns whenever they awaken. It will be days before she can leave them even for a little while.

From time to time, the father fox enters the den to sniff his new family. Most of his nighttime hours are spent searching for prey. After every successful hunt, he brings food to the den. Poking his head inside, he makes a soft warbling sound that tells his mate food has arrived. The female eats his offerings hungrily several times a night. It is very important for her to eat well and stay healthy so she can nurse her young. Without the father's help, the mother and her pups might not survive.

Within a few weeks, the pups' eyes have opened and the babies can walk and run. Growing fast, they are ready for solid food. The fox family abandons the nursery den. By day, they sleep in temporary hideouts called rallying points. At night, the growing pups learn to catch insects, mice, and earthworms by watching their parents. Pastureland is filled with earthworms. Developing the skill of tugging them from the ground without breaking them takes practice. But the pups catch on quickly and before long are eating as many as two hundred earthworms a night. Earthworms are an important part of a red fox's diet. They provide protein needed for strong muscles.

Much of the day, the pups concentrate on play. The father fox romps and tumbles with his youngsters. The pups sneak up and pounce on one another. Nearby, the mother watches and interrupts their play only if it

Red fox pups are ready to explore outside their den when they are just a few weeks old (above). Rough-and-tumble play helps the pups develop strong muscles and practice their skills as predators (left).

becomes too rough. This play is not all for fun. It is the way little foxes learn and practice their hunting skills. These childhood lessons will enable them to find enough food to stay alive when they are on their own.

By the end of the summer, the six-month-old foxes are ready to leave their family and live alone. Each may establish his or her territory just a few hundred yards from the others. In another year, each will be ready to seek a mate and raise its own pups.

Red foxes are found in a variety of wooded habitats and farmland throughout most of North America and Europe. Like other fox species, the adult red foxes are models for their young. Fox pups, like many hunting mammals, learn by watching and imitating their parents as they grow up.

The father red fox stays with his family and plays with the growing pups.

Cotton-Top Tamarin

It is just after sunrise when the family of cotton-top tamarins awakens—mother, father, and two sets of twins. The morning sun beams through the dawn mist in the Colombian rain forest. The family sleeps huddled together among the giant vines that wrap the tree branches. Here, twenty feet above the forest floor, the tamarins are well hidden from nighttime jungle predators. These squirrel-sized South American monkeys rarely come down to the forest floor. They find the food and water they need in the leafy branches.

The father tamarin stretches sleepily and pushes through the vines around him. He licks raindrops from the leaves to quench his thirst. Over his shoulder, four tiny eyes blink in the sunshine. His two-week-old twin daughters are clinging tightly to his shiny black fur. Already their heads and bodies are covered with short dark fur, and they have the white patches of hair that give the cotton-tops their name.

The mother and the older twins—a male and a female—poke their heads through the leafy vines and feel the warm, damp air. All six cotton-tops will spend the day climbing from tree to tree as they search for insects and fruit. Before nightfall, the family will be more than a mile from this spot. Tamarins do not return to the same nest site each night. At dusk, they find a new leafy hiding place where they can snuggle together.

With arms outstretched, the father squats on the limb and leaps toward a tree nearly ten feet away. Gliding gracefully, he grabs a limb. His piggybacking babies are still firmly attached. The twins twitter contentedly as

For the first few weeks of life, baby cotton-top tamarins cling to their father's back whenever they are not being nursed by their mother.

their papa pokes in the leaves and bark, searching for food. Nearby, the older youngsters and the mother find some ripe figs. They use their claws to pick the sweet, fleshy fruit. This favorite food is quickly gobbled up.

Suddenly, a scaly brown head pushes soundlessly through the leaves, and a black forked tongue flicks toward the monkeys. It is a large snake, hunting for prey. The father tamarin chirps loudly and jumps nervously from branch to branch. He leaps into the tangled vines on a nearby tree.

The mother and the older twins scream alarm calls before they dive after him. The cotton-tops have had a close call with a dangerous predator. These small monkeys must be careful, or they will become the prey of snakes, owls, hawks, or jungle cats.

The danger past, the cotton-top tamarins continue to make their way through the jungle branches. They often stop to rest. Sometimes one of the older twins carries its tiny sisters. Because the newborns are always kept together, they are quite a load to handle. When the babies get a little older, their brother and sister will play with them.

By midmorning, it is time for the younger twins to be fed. For the first month, the baby tamarins drink only their mother's milk. Although the father carries the babies much of the time, he gives the infants to their mother several times a day to nurse.

In about five weeks, the youngsters will no longer drink just milk. They will take fruit offered by their parents. Soon they will explore a little on their own. If something scares them, the little tamarins leap for the back of the nearest family member. The babies will be almost grown before the older tamarins refuse to carry them anymore.

Tamarin youngsters stay with their family for a year or two. Then they will leave to find mates from other tamarin families in the rain forest. Next year, their mother will give birth again. These unusual little monkeys almost always have twins, and the one-year-old sisters will care for the next newborns, just as their brother and sister cared for them.

Cotton-top tamarins are an endangered species. Only a few remain in the rain forests of Colombia, South America, and some are being raised in captivity. Unique among monkeys, tamarin behavior is a good example of the important job that certain fathers and family helpers have in caring for newborns. The mother would have an impossible job if she had to carry the babies while another set of twins was developing inside her. The father is a very important part of this family of care givers.

The father tamarin shares a piece of fruit with his nearly grown youngster.

Conclusion: The Next Generations

There are millions of animal species in the world today, from enormous whales to the tiniest of insects. All have special adaptations for survival that include some unique ways of helping the next generation get started.

Although baby reptiles, insects, and many other kinds of animals need no attention from their parents, other types of animal babies do. In some cases, both the mother and father have jobs that are essential for the survival of their young. When a father takes over certain exhausting, and sometimes dangerous, parenting duties, the mother's energy and often her life are saved. A healthy mother animal may be able to produce a large number of healthy youngsters. This new generation will carry on the species.

Mates for life, the mother and father bald eagle share the demanding job of feeding their growing youngsters.

Glossary

Adaptation—an animal's behavior or a particular body feature that helps it survive.

Brood—to nurture eggs or young.

Clutch—the eggs in a nest.

Courtship—behaviors that attract a male and female of the same species to each other.

Egg—a female reproductive cell.

Fertilize—to unite sperm with eggs for reproduction.

Fry—a newly hatched fish.

Hormone—a chemical that controls certain body activities.

Nymph—the immature stage in some insect life cycles.

Predator—an animal that kills other animals for food.

Prey—an animal killed and eaten by another animal.

Species—a kind of animal.

Sperm—a male reproductive cell.

Index

Photographs are in **boldface**.